Articles from the

New Physiocrats

The Rise of a New
Economic Philosophy

HTTPS://NEWPHYSIOCRATS.ORG

Table of Contents

Why Did We Form the New Physiocratic League?

We want to live in a world where everyone finds the entrepreneur inside themselves, and has the means to take risks. A world where people live for adventure. We want to live in a place that inspires, a place of great architectural beauty. And we want people to have the means and time to enjoy it. This is what we want for ourselves, and we want to share our dream with the world.

Manifesto of the New Physiocrats

Preamble

The cries for economic justice have become louder, and have rattled political establishments the world over. Housing has become unaffordable. Politicians offer easy answers and handouts, but no meaningful solutions. Meanwhile, the deep rot that underpins the current economic structure will continue to fester until the land beneath it finally collapses. Until we understand what the land is, we are at odds with everything we touch.

However, it is the land itself, and its treatment in economics, which is at the root of of this tumult. When one owns land, it is the location - the physical space - that is owned. The owner becomes a monopolist, and no one can gain the right to live on the said land without paying the monopoly price for rent. It is not the price of a competitive market.

Background

The entire increase in wealth inequality for the past decades is attributed to the unjust real-estate market.

The real estate market cycle is a primary cause of economic booms & busts.

Access to locations is critical for access to employment and amenities.

Wages earned from labour and entrepreneurialism are wages earned by individuals, while gains from land price increases are a result of nature & community.

Labour is currently taxed, with the proceeds spent on projects which inflate the gains of land-owners & speculators.

Free money, handouts, easy lending, and price controls, do not address supply constraints and purchasing power; they raise rents and decrease supply respectively.

The peculiarities of land such as its fixed supply can be applied to a select few other assets as well, but land is the especially critical due to its necessity for life.

Credit in the economy has been directed toward inflating land values rather than productive capital.

Shifting the tax burden towards land values, away from labour, is the first and most crucial step to correcting the imbalance.

We must beware those offering solutions that overlook land and supply issues.

What We Stand For

Respecting the differences between bounty gifted by nature, and that which is earned by our labour.

A positive rate of taxation on products of nature & community - for example land values, air [pollution]   with zero and negative rates of taxation on products of labour.

Seeking liberty; by expressing its ideals politically, and also by pursuing adventure, freedom, and knowledge in our own lives.

Justice, fairness, the resulting success by merit, and insisting it be reflected in the systems by which we're governed.

Absolute transparency in government.

Unifying the original Physiocratic-Geoist ideas with distilled wisdom of tradition and the reality of modernity.

Implementing a long-term vision rather than short-term reactions, and attempt to understand how such a vision may be remembered in history.

Recognizing that each individual and each group has its own distinct strengths, which must be capitalized-on in order to maximize opportunity within our economic ecosystem.

Exploring our world,, understanding it is ours to travel and learn from, and our responsibility to protect and be stewards of for future generations.

Defending individuals, cultures, economies, and environments from injustice.

Our Legacy

The original Physiocrats were a precursor to the later Georgism, which demonstrated the value of separating land (products of nature) from the other factors of production (labour and capital) when addressing policy. This long-known wisdom is a concept that was also touched upon by the Stoics and in imperial China. The New Physiocrats see how each iteration of the Geoist philosophy has developed, and have created the latest iteration as a comprehensive platform to unite Geoist organizations; intended to be applicable for the present and the future, with an emphasis on political feasibility.

This also includes ensuring our public physical space & architecture is that of great beauty. It also means a deep respect for private property, liberties, and one's labour & entrepreneurialism. These products of human labour should ideally have a zero or negative rate of net taxation, in order to amplify their expression. These products must be represented politically, and not crowded out by special interests. The New Physiocratic philosophy draws a morally consistent line between products of nature and products of labour, between public and private. Respecting these boundaries allows us to live within a consistent and integrated political philosophy, in harmony with nature at large, and within our own human nature.

Why a Land Value Tax is Inevitable

A decade after the late 2000s recession, much of the world is now back at the top of the economic cycle, and critically near the next crisis. At the top of an economic cycle, governments are collecting their peak tax revenue yet even so, many are still running large fiscal deficits and have large existing public debts. This includes the United States, Canada, and the UK among others.

With public finances in such a precarious situation, when the next recession hits, policymakers will be presented with dwindling options. Tax cuts and stimulus will be challenging, as the appetite for bond purchases by investors and central banks have already been stretched to their limits. This may be attempted, but especially with turbulence in global trade (affecting the supply of goods) and years of quantitative easing (affecting the supply of money), inflationary pressures would be too high to tolerate. In fact, one could argue that the consumer price index has already dramatically understated inflation with increases mostly accumulating in the real estate market, making housing unaffordable. Further monetary easing or fiscal stimulus would simply accrue more gains to the real estate market, due to land & tax policy which incentivize locations to be poorly used, monopolized, and prohibitively expensive. This is the Henry George Theorem, which demonstrates how government spending increases land values by more than this expenditure. Furthermore, the build quality, architecture, and locations of real estate projects have left much to be desired. Central banks are analogous to the driver of a car, but with so much of the lending injecting fuel into consumption and land speculation instead of more viable investment, it's as if we've had our foot on the gas pedal for 10 years but the engine is broken.

Raising tax rates presents yet still more problems. Capital (and perhaps labour) will either make efforts to avoid these taxes, or will outright flee. There will be less to tax, and tax increases will slow the economy. This will first be seen in the riskiest emerging markets that already run dual deficits and have no control over hot money inflows, such as Turkey and the Philippines (where we can expect a wave of defaults). Soon we will see that developed markets are not immune from outflows, depreciations, and bond sell-offs either. Raising taxes on capital or labour would worsen these problems in exactly that order, as well as both fiscal and current account deficits.

Years of debt-fueled consumption buoyed by a soon-to-be deflating real estate sector have left consumers stretched far too thin for a consumption-led recovery. Yet lending in many countries has skipped over investment in real production, which is where the monetary stimulus should have been flowing to all along. Poor tax policy has ensured that it did not.

What options will policymakers have to deal with the next crisis?

With government and consumer spending out of fuel, and no room for tax increases to plug the deficit (without tanking the economy), the first place policymakers will look, will be back to the central banks.

However, with central banks already stretched as well, they will have to become increasingly creative to achieve the same stimulative effect as before. This might mean outright and unsterilized monetization of debt. Some countries might still have room for such policies (which ones exactly will soon become clearer), however the majority will not be able to do so without severe inflationary consequences. Furthermore, if so little of the previous rounds of monetary easing resulted in productive investment, and instead led to unsustainable consumption, inflated asset prices, and property speculation, then more of the same rate cuts and quantitative easing will result in the same cycle once again. That is of course unless tax (and governance) reform addresses this.

The next place policymakers will look, will be to smaller government, and perhaps the unloading of obligations onto local governments. Improved governing efficiency and the streamlining of bureaucracy are absolutely necessary. However, the best time to take such actions is when the economy is running hot, so that the private sector can absorb laid off public-sector workers. If there hasn't been the political will to do so during times of growth, where will the political will be to take such measures during a recession? And if this is done during a recession, the expense of handling the unemployed will fall back again on government, especially with a population now drained of savings and mired in debt.

This leaves one final option: a shift in taxes on to unearned income, namely land value taxes (LVT). The LVT is not the same as a property tax, as it does not punish those who put the land to use; it taxes only the land, not the structure built on top of it. The benefits of LVT have been much discussed by famed economists across the political spectrum from Joseph Stiglitz to Milton Friedman. Unlike labour and capital, land cannot flee the country, or change in supply. It can be taxed without passing on price increases. It's highly transparent, as property cannot be hidden, and it's progressive most of the rise in wealth inequality can be attributed to land. However, most of all, it is one of the rare taxes that does not diminish economic activity, and in fact stimulates it. It lights fire under the feet of land speculators and those underusing large lots of valuable urban land, putting it to its highest and best use. It pushes more units of housing onto the market, making them more accessible and affordable. It can also be combined with other incentives, proposed by the New Physiocratic League in the form of ULT, to shape our towns, cities, architecture, housing, commute times, and amenities in the ways we desire.

Going back to the Henry George theorem, since increases in government spending (particularly in infrastructure) disproportionately raises land values, an LVT makes infrastructure spending self-funding. Tax receipts would rise as a result of the investment. It would even allow for a reduction in transit fares, the gains of which would be recollected from the LVT.

Shedding taxes on labour and capital, while shifting the burden onto land (and perhaps other unearned income) is the only way out of the fiscal hole that many nations have dug themselves into. It ensures credit flows into building homes, not hoarding land. By allowing for the removal of taxes on earned income, it producers higher net incomes and investment. By doing so, it is also the first and perhaps most crucial step in addressing current account imbalances, housing affordability, and economic injustice.

Is an LVT politically viable?

For a start, many governments will be left with no choice. Some might give the green light to central banks to attempt to cut debt by using inflation and monetization as a band-aid solution that will inflict tremendous pain, or will simply not succeed due to slowing monetary velocity. Those attempting half-hearted tax or spending reforms will run into walls from either increasing debt levels or the heavy burden of austerity.

The good news is, despite major resistance from certain lobbies, LVT is already making a comeback in the political realm for the first time since the early 20th century, before the memory of Henry George took a century-long hiatus from our collective minds. LVT has already been a success in the past in some localities in the US, Australia, and Asia. It has been within the scope of political discussion of officials in Asia recently, particularly in Thailand, Korea, and Taiwan, where some Georgist policies have already had success. Major political parties in the UK, both national and regional, have recently adopted the LVT as part of their platform, which gives a lot of hope that an LVT in the UK will come to fruition before the middle of the next decade, replacing more harmful taxes. A recession will hasten this change, due to a lack of other options to fund government. The UK will likely be the biggest testing ground for an LVT in the 2020s, from which we hope to learn a lot.

So while the 2020s will certainly inflict a lot of pain due to policy mistakes of the previous years, there is now hope that governments will be forced into long overdue corrections, which start with an LVT. Without it, sovereign defaults, hyperinflation, and depression, none of which mix well with the current global political environment, are the dangerous paths we don't want to take, as we have in the past.

The Renters' Revolt

January 1st 2025 felt like crossing into a milestone year. The stock markets reached new, stratospheric highs, not topped since 2018 - 2019. New & unconventional monetary policy, implemented after a rapid interest rate drop back to 0 was ineffective, helped avert calamity from the last recession. Property prices soared again, enriching some on paper, but leaving you an eternal renter. You weren't alone the balance of renters to homeowners had finally tipped in favor of renters as homeownership proved too far out of reach.

This time would be different, however. Different than 2019 when inflation was disguised mostly in asset prices. What seemed to be a future without inflation appearing in the CPI, proved to be only a momentary lapse, with a strong dollar sucking up relatively cheap imports. When the dollar sank as the current account and fiscal balance went over the edge, inflation rose, and even the most dovish in the Federal Reserve agreed it was time to raise rates dramatically.

All the while, various movements attempting to address rental price issues started gaining traction. Taxes on foreign property owners were politically popular, but had little effect on the supply of available units. Movements such as Deutsche Wohnen & Co Enteignen in Berlin, advocating outright nationalization of the housing supply were extreme and dangerous, but still made headway in cities with renters, even in neighboring countries. Switzerland, with its direct democracy, even collected enough signatures to put a similar proposal on the ballot. With the proportion of renters quickly rising in the UK, Ireland, Denmark, and the United States, the idea of a land value tax began to seem more politically realistic. Major British political parties had already campaigned for an LVT a few years prior, and Denmark already had one in place, albeit at a low rate.

Various groups long-advocating for an LVT managed to band together, and make a convincing case as an alternative for those pushing for nationalization and direct intervention. However, it wasn't until the following year when higher interest rates started to bite, collapsing the real estate market, when national governments were strapped for cash without the ability to monetize more debt and were left with few options. Lower fuel tax receipts as a result of electric cars left governments even-less able to pay off their infrastructure bills.

The UK and Denmark passed land value tax legislation, followed by the Swiss, and some German municipalities. North American cities later followed, beginning with Vancouver and NYC. Studies of little-known LVTs already in place in Asia, began to circulate, and Georgists in North America, Europe, Southeast Asia, Australia, and India started to connect further.

Would LVT rates be high enough to resolve economic imbalances before the 2030s? If a land value tax made headway, would the political movement get hijacked by those seeking nationalization and other various extreme or damaging policies? Would anti-LVT groups seeing the ineffectiveness of too-low an LVT rate pressure policymakers to scrap the idea? Would governments just use an LVT as another tax grab without reducing rates on productive activity, giving political fuel to anti-LVT'ers?

It's important we look to the future to see opportunities and potential allies. By the same token, it's important to see where conflicting ideologies and movements might be faster or more assertive to act. Most of all, it's important to synchronize and act in unison with concrete steps when looking at future scenarios.

Meet the People Rescuing American Politics by Trying to Capture Land Value

The US Democratic Party, at least according to their official platform, claims to be in favor of raising incomes, fighting for economic fairness, environmental justice, and quality education. They (like their opposition) have failed on all counts. Furthermore, their platform is moving further in the opposite direction, rehashing failed old ideas, and each day straying more from the policies that made America a land of opportunity for everyone. The Republican Party exhibits many of the same symptoms, just with different spending preferences.

For the newest generation of Democrats, the answer to America's biggest problems is big government. This means more opportunities for special interests and monopolistic firms to entrench their positions by protecting their regulatory regimes. It means large webs of complex programs with tremendous waste, in a time of growing deficits. To pay for expanding government, they offer economically dangerous and overly simplistic solutions, like taxing income earners and raising the minimum wage, without addressing any root causes. These approaches may make for good media sound bites, but ultimately harm the people they were intended to help. The truly rich don't pay income taxes like the majority do, and the biggest burden would instead fall on to doctors and much-needed professionals. Increased spending on marginalized groups do nothing to help the plight of the needy, as the structure of the economy and tax system allow any gains to get eaten up in rents, while subsidizing a broken society.

Evidence shows that increasing wealth inequality is almost entirely due to real-estate, a market which the young are priced out of, and is promoted as an investment vehicle rather than a place to live. Those who didn't buy in to the market years ago, can no longer afford to neither rent nor buy. Yet proposed tax increases would fall on hard-working income earners rather than location monopolists. The new left (nor the right) does not understand the difference between earned income, and wealth derived from nature, and therefore see a buoyant real estate market as a positive for the economy, and a ticket to easy riches. Understanding this is one key to understanding America's distorted economy, yet is not acknowledged by the major parties. Instead, both parties have used tax incentives and the allowance of uncontrolled monetary policy to inflate housing bubbles, and we've seen where this has led the economy.

The inequalities and injustices that the proposed government programs are meant to address, will only be worsened by them, just as they have been by the policies that preceded them. The complex regulations and subsidies that prevent new entrants from entering the upper echelons of banking, technology, and other restricted sectors of the economy, only serve to protect the incumbents. Under the administration of what could possibly be a socialist-leaning Democratic presidency, this red tape would surely increase, entrenching oligopolies.

Americans at the lower end of the income spectrum are forced into low quality schools in their neighbourhoods, without school choice. They then enter the labour force with skills worth less than the minimum wage, which politicians like Ocasio-Cortez want to raise to price even more workers out of the market. The middle class faces monopsony-like conditions in the labour market due to a lack of choice between employers, which hold on to their grip via regulation and lobbying for their interests, without the worry of startups attaining the same influence.

The solution to these issues is not burden professionals with more taxes, to raise the deficit, to fund programs with monetization, or to introduce multitude of bureaucratic programs. This is not the way the United States became the world's leading economy - a position that is slipping from its grasp. The solution is to allow competition to flourish again, to stop crushing entrepreneurs through regulation, to introduce choice in schools and public services, to replace bureaucratic programs and minimum wage laws with a path to supercharge wages, and to shift the burden of taxation away from human effort - instead onto land, environmental externalities, and products of nature. These are solutions which solve root causes of America's economic ills (and with moral/ideological consistency) as opposed to window dressings that worsen the problems.

Thankfully, there is a political action organization within the US Democratic Party which understands the root causes, and has a platform which begins to address them. The Democratic Freedom Caucus uses policies rooted in Georgism to propose real policy solutions. A shift away from income taxes toward land value taxation would immediately lift incomes and boost housing supply to lower costs. At the same time, the resulting better use of land would reduce transportation times and reduce the burden on the environment. Streamlining regulation and eliminating corporate welfare would not only reduce costs to consumers, but would grant new options to employees, allowing people to reach the better paying jobs they seek. Finally, introducing choice with regards to government services, means that children would not be relegated to inferior schools, and parents could instead choose the best possible options.

While the platform of the Democratic Freedom Caucus does have its differences to TNPL's, the New Physiocratic League views the DFC as the only savior to the Democratic party and perhaps to the American political direction as a whole. Organizations of liberty-minded Republicans might also be natural allies if they are receptive to the Geoist message.

The choices are between a Democratic Party that hands a win to the status quo by offering endless economic malaise and opportunities for rent-seeking and corporate welfare, and a Democratic Party that offers real solutions and finds potential allies across the aisle. At this critical political junction, now is the time to choose.

The Flag of the New Physiocratic League

The circle at the center of the flag consists of land (illustrated with a spade in its centre), integrated with an hourglass. This represents the public recapture of our time and space, in essence an expansion of Georgism, which focused primarily on space. The fusion of time and space as spacetime [in the realm of physics] became more widely discussed a bit later than Henry George's publication of Progress and Poverty.

The transparency of the hourglass in the centre makes a statement of transparency [in governance] at the core. The recognizable spade symbol, as a bettor might see in a deck of cards, also serves as positive recognition for the risk-taking nature of the entrepreneurs.

Combining the chain of DNA/cellular division with the gear, represents industry powered by our biology, and an encompassment of the flexible, evolutionary quality of nature. This alludes to Physiocracy's respect for nature itself, natural laws, the beauty of biological differences with the specializations it creates, and the organic nature of a functioning market economy. In essence, harnessing the power of human behavior and market economics to drive national industry.

Eight teeth in a gear, with eight notches, represent the 16 economic goals represented by the Sectoral Banks, of different weighting in governing influence. The three rings (from the inside moving out), represent the original factors of production: land, labor, and capital.

Land is represented by the sandy ring encircling the spade, the DNA/dividing cells representing human labor, and the gear representing capital. The shape of the four-layered symbol in its entirety mirrors the shape of the platform's proposed national parliament, with its four chambers.

The colors, brown with blue, were intended to represent land, air, and water. These are the elements of the earth that Physiocrats consider to have a public dimension, not created by human labor, and suitable for taxation.

These particular shades of the colors were used to create a feeling of majesty and tradition. Tradition, while not always a suitable advisor for the modern world, is a domain that the New Physiocrats appreciate as something to be considered (along with laws of nature), as a distillation of many years of lessons learned from history.

The respect of both science and tradition, new and old, urban and rural, symbolizes a reconciliation of two warring sides of the political spectrum.

We Can Shed Our Debts and Restore Prosperity. Look to the Land.

If you're reading this, there's a good chance that debt will impact your life in some way in the near future, and not for the better. Perhaps directly as a debtor, or perhaps indirectly, as we feel its effects throughout the broader economy.

Debt is not inherently bad. It can be used to invest and grow, whether it be a business or an economy. On the national or regional level, there are a lot of low hanging fruit in which debt can be utilized to produce long-term growth, especially when a country is in its early stages of development. In more developed countries this can still be done, but it becomes increasingly difficult. A country which has no infrastructure can build a railway, port, and road network to get its goods to markets. Individuals and firms want to move near this infrastructure, so land values nearby start to rise. Instead of collecting rents from the land owners who were lucky enough to benefit from these nearby projects, governments tend to unfairly burden the workers and entrepreneurs with these debts by taxing them. In the early stages of development, since these workers might benefit so much from the infrastructure, their increased incomes may be able to shoulder the burden. If land owners decide to use their land efficiently, for example, to support an adequate supply of housing, workers may be able to still use their after-tax incomes to rent or buy a home, and governments can then use their income tax revenues to repay the debts.

Lenders/bondholders get repaid and have the confidence to lend again in the future.

Reality, unfortunately, has not been so kind. Due to poor land usage, resulting from a combination of zoning laws, real estate speculation, and in particular, a lack of incentives to increase the supply of housing (and in many cases commercial or industrial space), workers and entrepreneurs are hit with a double burden. First with income taxes, and then again with the increase in real-estate prices resulting from the projects which their taxes and labour builds. When factoring in housing in purchasing power calculations, real incomes are being crushed. Credit tends to flow into land to chase its price gains rather into productive assets, worsening the issue. In developed countries, public projects often no longer pay the same kind of dividends to incomes as they do for countries in their early stages of development, as necessary as these projects may be. The remainder of these tax revenues may also go to fund an elaborate bureaucracy and web of programs of varying effectiveness, which have failed to raise the incomes of the majority to a degree which would compensate their burden.

Because incomes aren't rising adequately, there is less to tax (as the tax burden falls disproportionately on incomes). And because government projects are showing diminishing returns to prosperity, the fiscal deficits, in turn, only worsen. Trying to increase the burden on upper tax brackets or firms only drives money and labour to hide or flee, and unfairly targets much-needed skilled professionals such as medical practitioners, specialized tradespeople, and innovative entrepreneurs. Meanwhile, owners of expensive land (which would be far more transparent to tax and easier to account for) watch their property wealth rise at the expense of new property buyers or renters. The labour force is forced into debt to afford expenses (especially housing and consumer durables), and the financial sector profits off mortgages and the consumer debt that workers borrow to pay their bills.

In Canada, the US, UK, and Australia among many other countries, the current account balance has been deeply in the negative for an uncomfortably long time, indicating that these countries have been consuming more than they produce. These governments are running sizable fiscal deficits as well, only compounding the issue (of which it is often associated). Typically, countries facing a dual deficit scenario eventually face jarring currency depreciation, forcing a wrenching adjustment of the current account balance, at which point central banks to step in to raise interest rates to prevent an inflationary spillover. This usually also means a deep recession and involuntary fiscal discipline (both public and private) as credit dries up. This is the kind of painful correction that some say is needed, to reorient the economy and direct misused resources. Yet it doesn't address the fundamental issues with regards to the economy's incentive structure.

The tax system rewards the misuse of land which results in a lack of affordable real estate as its prices soar, and encourages the use of debt - especially mortgage and consumer debt. This is money that could have been channeled into savings, investment, and production. It would keep the current account in check and private debt levels sustainable. Unlike goods or typical assets, land cannot increase in supply in response to price rises, so instead of resulting in any positive effect, the end result is just a lack of affordability and access. The current account deficits, in part driven by this resulting lack of capital investment, are further enabled by the market distortion of subsidized goods from abroad, and an overvalued currency (as indicated by the dual deficits) aided by reserve-currency status, and in some cases, hot money inflows. The mispricing of goods and currencies is not the result of a functioning market, and instead aids in the misallocation of capital. Note that if these economies' tax structures were tilted more towards production and investment (and away from debt-fueled consumption) resulting in a rebalance of current accounts, the currency valuations would make more economic sense. The governments then tax money from workers and entrepreneurs which further reduces production by hampering productivity, reducing the ability to save and invest in even more production. As a result, the economy is heavily tilted towards unsustainable levels of consumption without the possibility of producing enough to compensate for it. Furthermore, workers are unjustly squeezed at every turn, and the more we work, the more we're taxed, and the more that tax money is either squandered or used for projects which ratchet up the price of already unaffordable real estate for which output-generating workers are not compensated for.

To restore the balance and reverse years of this damage, we need to reorient these economies to once again allow production to flourish, and allow capital to flow to its rightful places. However, this reorientation must be permanent, and not accomplished through repeated, violent crashes that follow the popping of unsustainable credit and asset bubbles which we've grown so accustomed to. Otherwise, we will instead repay debts through inflation and further squeezing workers through income taxation. By extension, under the current incentive structure, any recovery from the next recession will once again be a veneer of growth masked by more asset price bubbles, unaffordable real estate, and hidden inflation, as was with the previous recovery. Real prosperity must come from rising production, total factor productivity, and broad-based income growth that doesn't rely on excessive consumer nor public debt.

The only way to get out of the fiscal deficit hole without sinking the economy is through the taxation of land values. In fact, a land value tax (LVT) is the only tax that can stimulate economic growth, rather than strangle it. At the same time it improves housing affordability by ensuring land goes to its highest and best use, and justly compensates the public for the monopoly on location. It is transparent, as land cannot be hidden offshore. By raising revenues through land, it also affords us to return income taxes back to the people, and even underwrite wages/labour (and capital) - as opposed to using arbitrary minimum wage laws and bureaucratic government programs that are currently required to support our most vulnerable under our current economic regime. Finally, an LVT rewards governments for smart investments, as investments which make the surrounding land more desirable are recouped through an LVT, perhaps with a profit.

Through the platform of the New Physiocratic League, the tax burden falls on land and the work of nature, of which we did not produce ourselves. Instead of taxing the efforts of workers and entrepreneurs, our incomes, savings, and investments are instead amplified under this platform. We would also be compensated for the use of our shared resources. Instead of using bureaucratic programs to apply band-aids to a broken system, automatic mechanisms would ensure that incomes, savings, investments, and production are absolutely maximized, while nature's bounty is shared, protected and compensated for. Such a system is not only one of economic justice, but is the only way to address unsustainable dual deficits, unequal opportunity, unaffordability, underproduction, exaggerated debt cycles, and environmental abuse in one elegant solution.

The New Physiocratic League platform can be summed up in 6 points:

Negative net taxation on personal incomes/savings (Three Pillars program)

Negative net taxation on business (Sectoral Banks program)

Tax products of nature and land value, NOT productive property

Tax consumption, NOT production

Replace bureaucracy with our proposed automatic mechanisms

Long-term vision instead of impromptu fixes

Modern Georgism

Georgism is modernizing to become more relevant. Not in the sense that the Georgist philosophy itself is any less relevant than before - in this sense it is more relevant than ever. Artificial economic growth balanced atop teetering mortgages, wealth inequality that's primarily a result of real estate prices, the unjust, inefficient use of physical space, the ease with which labour & capital flee from its unjust taxation, and tax systems that hold back the economy's potential are among some of current issues which Georgist policy addresses better than any other. However, Georgism as a relevant force in the media and mainstream political sphere, is showing green shoots. It is modernizing in the sense that there are a growing number of online media channels to educate the public on its virtues, and journalists in mainstream publications are picking up the Georgist storyline as well.

Georgist policy has an unusual ability to infiltrate existing and mainstream political parties, because the land value tax in particular can appeal to the left, right, and environmental parties. Petitioning government representatives is one effective way to bring Georgist policy into the mainstream, but it's most effective when mobilizing larger numbers. No one has since been able to match George's ability to mobilize those who want to see these policies in place.

It seems this is now starting to change. Over the past few years, there has been a noticeable uptick in Georgist activity. Georgists have opened more avenues to communicate and spread the message. The community has put more effort into online media, and the attention received is rising. Major media outlets including The Economist, Bloomberg, FT, and others, have been picking up stories related to Georgism and LVT with more frequency. We should take a moment to acknowledge the hard work that the community has put in to these goals, and to applaud them. The community has started to modernize thanks to your efforts and your engagement with the digital world.

The Georgist community is as fractured as others in some ways, each of us with our own nuanced political preferences. The New Physiocratic League tries to unify the community with a modernized platform focused on political feasibility and expanding on Georgist philosophy, as well as symbols/flag, colour scheme, and branding image. Perhaps not all agree. However, I think it's safe to say that most Georgists agree on the basics:

Replacing other taxes with the taxation of land value

Rewarding effort rather than taxing it

Acknowledging (as we had in the past) that land is a distinct factor of production, and is a product of nature rather than labour

A large proportion also agree that other natural resources such as air, electromagnetic spectrum, and waterways might also fall under the classification of land / common property. As to what extent an LVT can [politically] realistically replace other taxes, or to what extent this is desired, is where some in the community are divided. For example, The New Physiocratic League proposes cutting and flattening tax rates on incomes dramatically, and paying the rest of income tax revenues out as cash payments to all those in the labour force, to replace more complex and inefficient social programs. Some find this proposal too libertarian for their taste, or too far from George's single-tax proposal - while others not enough.

However, almost all of us in the community can agree on the most basic, main points. After all, that's what brought us together. Perhaps the Georgist umbrella organizations can acknowledge the different wings that the community has created, while at the same time highlight the basic policies we're aiming for. As long as we stick to the simple message, word will continue to spread. I'd like to thank the community for such amazing efforts, and for producing such informative, interesting, and share-able content, and inspiring us to continue on this path.

How the Three Pillars of Income Support Would Revive Depressed Regions

Around the world, the exodus from rural areas into cities has seemed unstoppable. In much of the developed world, this is a process that has mostly been completed. At the same time, de-industrialized cities face their own exodus, into the service-oriented cities. Populations have become concentrated towards hubs, and government efforts to redistribute production (and government offices) more evenly throughout countries, has been piecemeal, expensive, and ineffective.

There are no doubt plenty of advantages to megacities. Concentrated populations allow for the free flow of ideas, and provide opportunities with large markets and endless choices. Yet we fail to question the limits to scale, and the consequences of this change. The loss of rural towns, and an emptying of human capital from former-industrial cities also represents a loss of rural and working-class cultures, and contributes to a lack of affordable housing in growing cities while under-utilizing the excess resources of shrinking ones. Furthermore, small farms producing interesting, regional food products are become lost in favour of large monoculture farms, or under-utilized (and in some cases abandoned) rural land. A concentration of population centers amounts to a loss of diversity.

A land value tax is part of the solution. It prevents hoarding of land, pushes it towards its highest and best use, and improves its distribution among the population. It is also part of the solution to making megacities more affordable and accessible, especially if combined with a lifting of development-inhibiting regulations.

It is important to note how despite how the migration to megacities inflates their living costs, while costs fall in depressed regions, this cost difference is not enough to stem the flow of migration. The lower living costs in many regions are offset by fewer opportunities, or opportunities that pay far less. There are also separate issues such a lack of transportation infrastructure, lack of amenities, and activities, which drive people to move - which are partly addressed by the taxation of land by raising infrastructure funds and encouraging density and business activity.

The New Physiocratic League's proposal for a Three Pillars system of income support (which includes a National Dividend, National Income Supplement, and Assisted Savings Program) calls for a system in which earners within each of a country's income brackets benefit from each others' success. It calls for returning/distributing all personal income taxes back to wage earners (those earning average incomes would receive the full amount, and those earning below would receive a pro-rated amount), all capital gains taxes to the population's savings/investment accounts (part of a mandatory savings program), and provides a dividend from property of the commons. This means that as the incomes of one income bracket rises, those in the others rise along with it. It underwrites labour costs while amplifying incomes, and ensures that even those living in depressed communities see their incomes rise automatically. It would then become advantageous to live in low-cost regions. The New

Physiocrats call for a similar program to return corporate income taxes.

Of course, returning those tax revenues back to the people, is only possible with a form of land value tax in place to fund government operations (the New Physiocratic League proposes a ULT variation of this). A land value tax also ensures that the increases in personal incomes are not absorbed as rent, and is instead invested in the community.

The combination of land value taxation and the Three Pillars of income support ensure that those living in any part of a country can enjoy the benefits of the country's success. It does so without the need for complex, bureaucratic programs, and without running a deficit. Furthermore, it ensures that the market forces which would encourage people to live in lower cost regions, can do so effectively. Rural areas and de-industrialized cities would see an injection of new activity and prosperity.

Note: Regarding the point on LVT being only part of the affordability solution - artificial housing supply constraints due to zoning laws need to be addressed. An LVT should push land into productive use, and by extension increase the supply of housing, but it faces another hurdle with regulation. Removing or reforming these regulations is the other piece of the puzzle.

The idea behind the Three Pillars is to replace the labour market's straightjacket built out of minimum wage laws, heavy distortions, and complex, bureaucratic, means-tested welfare programs. I would imagine it would be a tough sell, politically, to remove these programs without replacing them. This program is intended to be a replacement. The Three Pillars is part of a simple direct cash-transfer system that would be automatic, deficit-free by design, and would effectively just make people's individual income tax rates either negative or approaching zero.

Furthermore, since it would be paid out as a percentage of one's earned income (e.g. someone earning the average national wage would receive the full amount, while those earning less would receive a pro-rated amount), it just amplifies existing wages, instead of reducing incentives to work.

Kyrgyzstan—An Economic Rising Star

We landed in Bishkek, Kyrgyzstan, with the usual hopes of finding adventure and opportunity. Expectations were muted after seeing so many far-flung places before which held so much promise, but didn't deliver. To my surprise, Kyrgyzstan would be different.

The plane touched down in Bishkek's Manas International Airport at 04:00, which was dated but functional. The drive into the city center began with a smooth new tree-lined road, which apparently was built the previous year in preparation for the Nomad Games. The streets of Bishkek were well-lit and organized, and the buildings reminiscent of a 1970s USSR but with a touch more neon lighting. It was exciting to see highway signs pointing to silk road cities such as Tashkent and Almaty, stirring up ideas for an exotic road trip.

The intersection of history and geography in Kyrgyzstan is part of what makes it a place of such intrigue and opportunity. As a former-Soviet republic, the Russian influence is very evident, with the widespread use of the Russian language, Cyrillic alphabet, and Soviet architecture. Its large border with China shines through in its cuisine, with hand-pulled noodles and meat-filled dumplings as a delicious starting point to experience Kyrgyzstan's culinary offerings. The 24/7 energetic spirit of the city with seemingly no rules on opening hours, and pubs continuing to serve food and drinks well after sunrise, reaffirmed that I was indeed in Asia. This was certainly no sleepy, quiet city. A visit to Osh Bazaar, and to Tzum - a sort of flea market built as a mall - highlights a deeply ingrained trading culture like you would find in Turkey. Even the heavy hand of communism could not dampen the Kyrgyz entrepreneurial spirit. Osh Bazaar is overflowing with exotic spices and dry fruit, and the sellers understand commerce and salesmanship. Unlike in other parts of the former communist world, the Kyrgyz people understand customer service, and the treatment received as a customer was always exceptional.

Scenery and nature are major highlights for most visitors to Kyrgyzstan. Lake Issyk Kul, a few hours from the capital, is the world's second-largest alpine lake. At nearly 6300 square kilometers, the lake is dotted with towns around its perimeter, and buzzing with life and a sense of emerging regional tourism. I have no doubt that this will increase in the future, but I hope it does not spoil the charm of the place. The country is mountainous, and the beautiful snow capped peaks could be mistaken for the Swiss alps. Within 45 minutes of Bishkek you can climb some of them at Ala Archa national park. There is even a developed ski resort at Karakol, overlooking Lake Issyk Kul.

Something must be said about the Kyrgyz people, their openness, and their hospitality. It wasn't possible to go for more than an hour without experiencing it. Stopping to look at a map invites people to come help you find directions. The locals are interested in visitors, and were always enthusiastic to show us around, while refusing anything in return. At one point I stopped at a busy bakery to pick up some pastries and a man insisted on buying us all the available offerings. He then offered a hug and sent us on our way with his best wishes.

The energy of the locals extends to the country's nightlife, with an emerging culture of microbreweries, experimental pubs, and clubs - many of which never seem to close, and are busy even on weeknights. As far as the outskirts of the small town of Balykchy, a roadside restaurant called Shafran turns into a disco after 9pm. This seems to be a recurring theme in Central Asia, and if a restaurant has two floors, the upper floor is bound to have music and dancing after a certain hour. This is a very far cry from the quiet conservatism of countries like Azerbaijan or the defeated feelings of perpetual depression in Moldova.

There is a small but tight-knit ex-pat community in Bishkek, including quite a few westerners, who are also convinced by Kyrgyzstan's prospects. Some are working for the local universities, and while they only intended to stay a short time, have ultimately extended their stay for the past 4–5 years and longer. Others are there for business, including one who shared his fascinating experience in starting a [soon-to-be] chain of restaurants in Central Asia, which began in Bishkek. Several others were of a similar mindset, and had been accelerating the growth of internationally-minded bars and cafes in Kyrgyzstan.

Part of the attraction of Kyrgyzstan is that it is the only democracy in the region. While the other "Stans" are under firm control of legacy political leadership from Soviet times, and neighbouring China maintains single-party rule, the Kyrgyz people have ousted presidents when there have been concerns of rigging, and continue to hold democratic elections (including the most recent one in 2017). It's worth mentioning that these alternative systems might be producing stability and positive results, and that our visit to neighbouring Kazakhstan showcased a thoroughly modern, developed, and impeccably clean country with growing oil, agricultural, and financial sectors. However, the openness of Kyrgyzstan has definitely attracted many creative thinkers and scrappy entrepreneurs.

Kyrgyzstan offers the most attractive tax regime in the region, and the lowest tax burden in the Eurasian Customs Union (EACU), with a flat 10 percent rate on both personal and corporate income. The free-floating currency with an absence of capital controls allow the domestic economy, which is heavily dependent on trade, to naturally adjust to shocks, and without impediments to capital flows for business. The Kyrgyz and Russian Cyrillic alphabets are relatively easy to learn, and this lends itself to an easier path of commerce straight to China's doorstep.

The economy of Kyrgyzstan has seen GDP growth average more than 4 percent for the previous few years, with growth expected to slow somewhat for 2018–19. However, this has been achieved recently with low inflation (3.2% in 2017 and 0.4% in 2016). During this period, the current account deficit decreased significantly. The fiscal deficit is covered by foreign aid, and should continue to recede as the technical acumen of the tax authorities improves. One point to note, is that in 2017, Kyrgyzstan's land registration services were recognised by the World Bank's Doing Business Report as among the best in the world. This makes the country especially conducive to a shift in the tax burden towards a land value tax, away from income tax, were this to be on the political agenda. The government's fiscal concerns make the transparency of an LVT even more attractive. In turn, this highlights the possibility to promote The New Physiocratic League platform in Kyrgyzstan.

Kyrgyzstan is still a relatively low income country, with a GDP per capita adjusted for PPP still under $4000, which means ample room for growth. It also has not suffered from an overvalued currency and Dutch Disease, which has afflicted some of its resource-rich neighbours. Its companies are privately held, as one of the earliest post-Soviet reformers, and its publicly listed companies, rumour has it, have shockingly low PE ratios.

Sandwiched between rapidly growing China and wealthy Kazakhstan, and given the outstanding qualities this country has, one might expect stronger growth from Kyrgyzstan. The free movement of goods, capital, and labour that the EACU provides should promote convergence of economic output, while Kyrgyzstan's border with China and the attractive Kyrgyz tax regime should provide further impetus for growth. The mountainous terrain indeed creates some challenges for development, however it would not be the first nation to carve out a prosperous alpine home. Perhaps it is just a matter of time and marketing before the world turns its eye to this gem of a country. Or perhaps its landlocked position necessitates an even deeper expansion of sound policy to ensure its prosperity.

Kyrgyzstan has the essential ingredients for a prosperous future, and we would like to see the platform of The New Physiocratic League implemented to ensure that it happens. These are policies which also ensure that the prosperity is accompanied by a preservation of the beautiful culture, environment, and way of life - all of which make Kyrgyzstan so precious.

The New Physiocratic Platform

Platform Principles:

- Tax products of nature and land value, NOT taxes on productive property, using other taxes only in case land value taxation is inadequate" (see ULT)

  - With an allowance local governments and regions to incentivize local architectural guidelines to showcase their culture

- To the extent any other taxes might be needed, there should be negative net taxation on personal incomes/savings (see our Three Pillars), to replace an ineffective and bureaucratic welfare system; and negative net taxation on productive business (see Sectoral Banks), giving small business a voice, and to mitigate against the weaponization of trade; use progressive consumption taxes (see Ben Cardin's PCT) as a backup, NOT taxes on production – to preserve the fiscal balance in the face of an aging population, and to reverse the artificial distortions that tilt the economy toward consumption over production & savings

- End corporate welfare & reverse economic distortions

  - eliminating subsidies, bailouts, uncompensated environmental use, special licenses, privileges, and other means of rent seeking and monopolization

- Absolute transparency

  - including the strongest possible anticorruption measures, an open land registry, and budgetary transparency

- Replace bureaucracy with automatic mechanisms (see our Automatic Mechanisms)

- Long-term vision instead of impromptu fixes (see our Platform and book)

Economic Reform

- Recognizing that land value taxation is the least harmful tax and that taxes on products of human effort should be minimized

- A shift away from taxes on earned incomes, towards taxes on unearned incomes (land, environment, and negative externalities)

- Return our income tax and magnify our wages through the introduction of a National Income Supplement, which is part of the New Physiocrats "Three Pillars" programs

- Extend the National Income Supplement to include homemakers and the short term unemployed

- Return corporate tax revenues back to business via Sectoral Banks, an automatic mechanism in the New Physiocratic economy

- Return Capital Gains tax back to the markets through Assisted Savings Program (ASP) accounts

- Replace state-pensions with ASP accounts (one of the Three Pillars), to magnify peoples' savings and investments

- Give all citizen-residents a share in the nation's unearned & natural wealth through a National Dividend (one of the Three Pillars)

- Replace minimum wage laws with the New Physiocrats' Three Pillars programs of direct cash transfers

- Replace an over-regulated labor market with maximum flexibility, training, and income security

- Implementation of a Unified Location Tax (ULT) to encourage rapid development with a focus on Basic Essentials and stunning architecture

- Employ powerful incentives to encourage long-term thinking throughout the economy and government

- Introduction of new management incentives to guarantee fair pay from employers

- Democratization of physical and visual space with an allowance for local governments to incentivize their local architectural guidelines and regional style

- Entrench rights to private property and earned income

- Introduce permanent institutions to lead a substantial effort to increase peoples' purchasing power, by driving down the cost of Basic Essentials

- Achieve greater self-reliance and broad economic diversification by reversing economic distortions with the use of Sectoral Banks

- Constitutional fiscal rules on spending, taxation, monetary policy, and deficits, to minimize public debt and eliminate corrupt/influential spending during election periods

- Introduce a constitutional government taxation and spending cap at a percentage of GDP, not including taxes/transfers from the Three Pillars program

- Introduce constitutional limits on state ownership, direct intervention, and bailouts; ensure it's consigned to the initial phase of introducing the New Physiocratic platform

- Employ a program to maximize the dispersal of labor market information, such as wages and job availability

- Mandate that industry sectors, under Sectoral Banks, each have their own training programs which ensure employment

- Create an employer of last resort, to provide temporary employment in public works when all else fails, and to prevent an overextension of monetary/fiscal policy to achieve political goals

- Tax short term capital inflows, with the revenues funding ASP accounts and Sectoral Banks

- Introduce a bill of rights for business, including maximum time limit on registering a business, and protections for private property and against injustice

- Replace both protectionism and unfair trade practices with the New Physiocrats' Compensatism, to ensure compensatory measures are applied evenly and not granting special privileges (compensating for unethical and anti-market practices, including slave labour, endemic subsidies & distortions, and large scale environmental destruction. It is in contrast to protectionism, which serves a different purpose, and ultimately tends to promote rent-seeking firms. Any compensation would have to be rules-based and applied evenly rather than being sector-specific)

- Eliminate planned obsolescence through packaging information, tax incentives, and introducing ratings and awards for durability

- Far-reaching monetary reform to prevent unsustainable debt levels

- Grant the central bank with a wider array of monetary tools, accompanied by better metrics to target to prevent the reliance on debt-inducing interest rate levers and QE. Ensure that it's rules-based and automated rather than discretionary, similar to a k-percent rule.

(It is our belief that inflation measures are too narrow, that inflation has been hidden in large asset-price increases, and that in part because of this, debt has spiraled out of control. We think debt levels should be a closer followed metric when it comes to central banks' mandates. It is also our view that capital requirements should be greatly increased, as an alternative to the current policy of over-regulation, which has worked just to stifle competition and entrench the current players in the market, creating large, shaky, uncompetitive banks with tremendous systemic risk.)

- Protect central bank independence allowing it to meet its new targets without political interference

- Introduce a 30-hour work week, with an official effort to maximize the population's free time, while freeing/deregulating the labour market so that it can clear effectively. Working hours can be reduced by replacing rules on hours of operation and introducing flexibility. Additional hours would be paid as overtime.

- Streamline bankruptcy courts and cap wait times for cases

- Introduce the South Korean model of net neutrality and network infrastructure

- Enhance urban density through the ULT

- Prioritize smart grids and cutting edge infrastructure, with targets to minimize commute times, maximize free time for the population, and create a real market for energy

- Limits and targets on regulatory and compliance costs for small business, included in the bill of rights for business

- Introduce targets to maximize the dispersal of information to ensure a functioning market

- Ending licenses as much as possible, and creating rules to ensure they don't reappear to create a means for special interests and oligopolies to emerge

Political Reform

- Introduce the most comprehensive and effective crackdown on corruption and waste in history, and create permanent anti-corruption & audit institutions to solidify the progress

- Tremendous simplification of bureaucracy and introduction of e-governance to replace the vast majority of paperwork

- Practice the utilization of policies based on empirical evidence, adapting governance policies from other nations achieving the best results

- Give official weight in government institutions to the importance visual space, particularly architecture

- Change to a quadriacameral legislature, which acts as a forum for individuals, economic sectors, and societal sectors to work together to meet the nation's goals

- Ensure that the interests of long-term thinking and elimination of corruption and waste have significant representation in parliament

- Enshrine the independence of the judiciary into the constitution, as a prerequisite to economic reform

- Ensure multi-purposing of military spending (e.g. for scientific, educational, and development purposes) to reduce waste

- Ensure that proposed policies can be devolved to the local level

Social Reform

- Official policy to respect and learn from history and tradition

- Complete legalization, regulation, and taxation of drugs and prostitution

- Publicly funded schools with vouchers, where students can choose their school instead of being tied to one district

- Replace summer holidays in schools with a form of national service to gain a sense of exploration as well as locational and social mobility

- Recognize the role of marriage in the current age demographic crisis

- Comprehensive marriage reform to ensure a more lasting union, and with fairness and justice being a top priority

- Recognize the valuable role of those who choose to raise children at home, and expanding the National Income Supplement to them

- Constitutional respect for free speech, expanding it to all public property including universities / education facilities

- Compensation for infringements on privacy such as big data to contribute to the national dividend

- Immigration policy focused on bringing in those who are needed and desired, rather than clouded by age demographic needs

- Introduce a New Physiocratic "Progress Index" as a new principal metric for success, alongside usual GDP and unemployment measures, complementing the economic reform

- Allow school choice with a voucher system (for schools which meet standards) to ensure every child can attain the best possible education regardless of background

- Strong constitutional support for civil liberties

Recommended Reading

http://evonomics.com/josh-ryan-collins-land-economic-theory/
How Land Disappeared from Economic Theory by Josh Ryan-Collins

https://www.reddit.com/r/newphysiocrats/comments/8x1fnl/upcoming_plans_for_the_new_physiocratic_league/
Upcoming plans for The New Physiocratic League

https://www.youtube.com/watch?v=j00ui5ue34E&feature=youtu.be
New Physiocratic League Intro Video

https://www.reddit.com/r/newphysiocrats/comments/942xfo/upcoming_plans_for_the_new_physiocratic_league/
Upcoming plans for The New Physiocratic League - Part 2

https://www.economist.com/briefing/2018/08/09/the-time-may-be-right-for-land-value-taxes
The time may be right for land-value taxes - The Economist

https://moneyweek.com/495610/its-time-to-reshape-our-beleaguered-housing-market/
The death of buy-to-let property is a useful cautionary tale for all investors

https://www.bloomberg.com/news/features/2018-10-20/vancouver-is-drowning-in-chinese-money
The City That Had Too Much Money

https://markets.businessinsider.com/news/stocks/the-new-physiocratic-league-endorses-innovative-uk-political-party-1027882627
The New Physiocratic League Endorses Innovative UK Political Party

https://www.strongtowns.org/journal/2019/3/4/you-get-what-you-tax-for
You Get What You Tax For

https://www.reddit.com/r/newphysiocrats/comments/axvfml/georgist_image_branding_and_culture/
Georgist Image, Branding, and Culture

https://www.reddit.com/r/newphysiocrats/comments/az9esk/groups_we_can_reach_out_to/
Groups We Can Reach Out To

https://babel.hathitrust.org/cgi/pt?id=wu.89100388719;view=2up;seq=2;skin=mobile
The Ralston-Nolan Bill - for a Land Value Tax

http://thelandcollective.com/a-policy-bringing-economists-and-urban-planners-together
A Policy Bringing Economists and Urban Planners Together

https://www.bloomberg.com/opinion/articles/2019-03-26/if-you-can-t-afford-the-rent-it-s-my-problem-too
If You Can't Afford the Rent, It's My Problem, Too by Tyler Cowen

https://markets.businessinsider.com/news/stocks/meet-the-people-launching-some-of-the-first-georgist-political-parties-in-decades-1027541467

Meet the People Launching some of the First Georgist Political Parties in Decades